CHANGING THE WORLD
ONE KITCHEN AT A TIME

A SERIES PRESENTED BY
CHILDREN'S CULINARY INSTITUTE

"Cooking may be as much a means of self-expression as any of the arts."
- Fannie Farmer

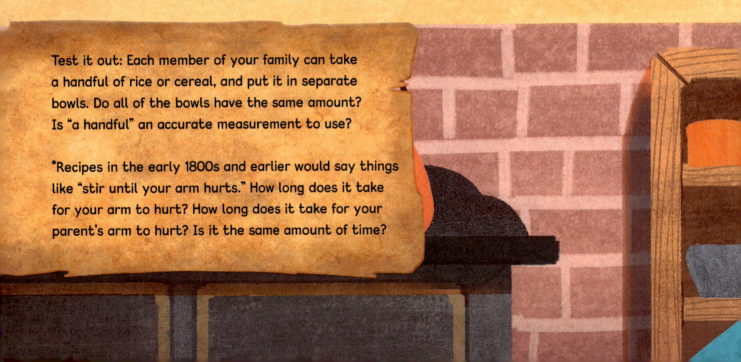

A long time ago, recipes were passed down in families from one generation to the next. The recipes were hand-written, and would list measurements such as "a pinch" of salt, "a handful" of flour, or "two thumbs" of butter. It is no surprise that when different people made the recipe, the taste and the texture were not the same.

Test it out: Each member of your family can take a handful of rice or cereal, and put it in separate bowls. Do all of the bowls have the same amount? Is "a handful" an accurate measurement to use?

*Recipes in the early 1800s and earlier would say things like "stir until your arm hurts." How long does it take for your arm to hurt? How long does it take for your parent's arm to hurt? Is it the same amount of time?

Today we have scales, dry measuring cups and spoons, liquid measuring tools and more. This helps us to be sure we get exact measurements, and that we make the recipe the way it is supposed to taste.

Can you find these tools in the picture?
- Sifter: to help break up lumps in powder ingredients for more even measurements
- Measuring Spoons: for small measurements
- Liquid Measuring Cup: usually has a spout for easy pouring, as well as lines to indicate amounts

Companies that package butter will often print measurements on the wrapper so the exact amount needed can be cut right off the stick.

Who makes the rules for how much flour makes a perfect cake, or how wide streets should be? Who decides which is the safest way to build a house, or how strong a bridge should be in order to hold a lot of cars?

Civil engineers design roads and streets, fire protection engineers create fire codes that keep us safe, and food engineers help us understand how we can cook tasty food safely. Do you think you would like to be a food scientist when you grow up?

Building codes are sets of rules that establish construction standards. Buildings and other structures must conform to these codes in order for builders to get permission to begin construction. This permission usually comes from a local governing council.

Fannie Farmer was born in March of 1857 in Boston, Massachusetts. Fannie's father was a master printer. Her family wasn't rich, but they valued education, and hoped to be able to send Fannie and her three younger sisters to college when they were old enough.

In 1855, the University of Iowa became the first public state university in the United States to teach both men and women.
Printing presses were used in the 1850s to make books, newspapers, and magazines.
This was the job of Master Printers.

When Fannie was sixteen and not yet finished with high school, she had a stroke which was most likely caused by Polio. She spent many years at home in bed recovering and learning how to walk again. The plans that Fannie and her parents had for her to go to college were not realised.

In the late 1800s, the United States experienced its first polio epidemic. An epidemic is the rapid spread of a disease to a large number of people in a given area over a short period of time. Polio, short for poliomyelitis, is a harmful disease caused by the poliovirus. If not treated, this virus spreads from person to person, and can cause paralysis, meaning the inability to move parts of the body. Sadly, many people have even died from the disease.

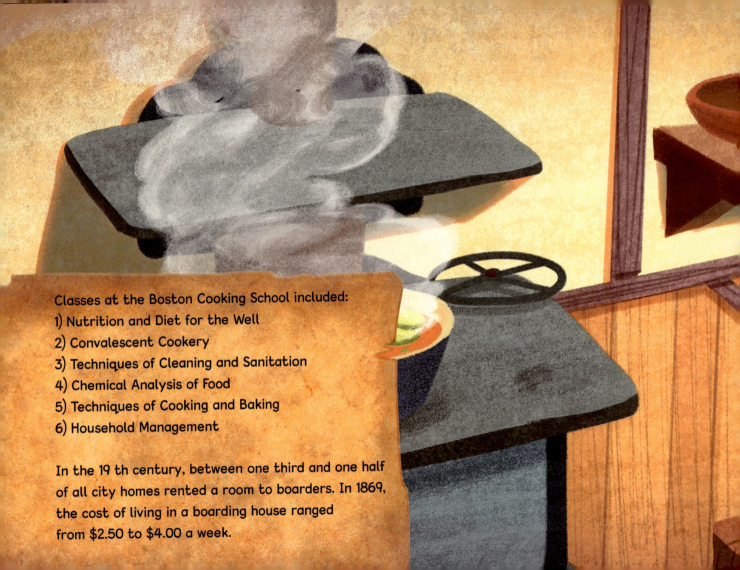

Classes at the Boston Cooking School included:
1) Nutrition and Diet for the Well
2) Convalescent Cookery
3) Techniques of Cleaning and Sanitation
4) Chemical Analysis of Food
5) Techniques of Cooking and Baking
6) Household Management

In the 19th century, between one third and one half of all city homes rented a room to boarders. In 1869, the cost of living in a boarding house ranged from $2.50 to $4.00 a week.

As soon as she could walk, Fannie took up cooking as a hobby, and did so well at it that she turned her parents' home into a boarding house. It became famous for the wonderful foods that she served, so they always had guests!

At the age of thirty, Fannie was encouraged to attend the Boston Cooking School. Fannie still had a limp from her childhood illness, but she persevered, and learned kitchen science. She was one of the star students, and when she graduated in 1889, she became an assistant to the director of the school.

A conference attended by a group of educators working together to elevate the discipline of kitchen and home sciences into a legitimate profession met in 1899. Originally, they wanted to call this profession oekeology, the science of "right living." However, the term home economics was ultimately chosen.

To "level off" means to remove any excess dry ingredients, so that they are level or even with the rim of the cup or top of the spoon. This ensures the measurement is accurate.

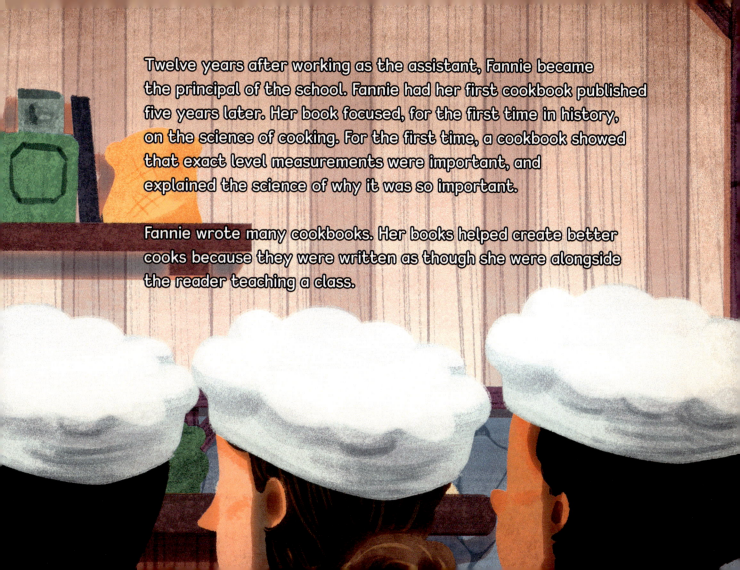

Twelve years after working as the assistant, Fannie became the principal of the school. Fannie had her first cookbook published five years later. Her book focused, for the first time in history, on the science of cooking. For the first time, a cookbook showed that exact level measurements were important, and explained the science of why it was so important.

Fannie wrote many cookbooks. Her books helped create better cooks because they were written as though she were alongside the reader teaching a class.

*Fannie was invited to lecture at the Harvard Medical School, and she began teaching convalescent diet and nutrition to doctors and nurses. She felt very strongly about the significance of proper food for the sick.

Fannie eventually opened her own cooking school called "Miss Farmer's School of Cookery." Her favorite subject was healthy cooking for people who were ill. Since she was so passionate about cooking to help people, she was often asked to lecture about it.

Fannie was a pioneer in the field of food science. She continued to teach, write, and even lecture about the science of cooking until she was fifty-seven. She has given home cooks and the culinary world a better understanding of the field, as well as the importance of precise measurements.

Baked Custard

2 eggs at room temperature
3 tablespoons granulated sugar
1/8th teaspoon salt
1 1/2 cups of milk
nutmeg

Slightly beat eggs, add sugar, salt and milk. Combine the mixture and strain into a greased pie plate. Sprinkle the top with ground nutmeg. Bake in a quick oven (425 degrees) at first (about 8-10 minutes) to set rim, decrease the heat (350 degrees) to allow eggs and milk to cook at a lower temperature. (finished when the custard has firmed to only a slight jiggle when shaken)

Experiment :

Make the recipe exactly as it is written then try some other changes to understand better how the recipe was tested and written this way. What are the differences in taste and texture?

Try:
*Using cold eggs
*Do not strain it before putting it in the baking dish
*Make it with eggs you have whipped for 3-5 minutes

What is a "quick oven"
The term "quick" oven comes from the time when wood-burning stoves without temperature gauges were the most common ones in kitchens

About Children's Culinary Institute

Children's Culinary institute is a program that teaches avid home cooks how to reach out into their communities and to teach children kitchen skills. We operate with our highest goal being the creation of a brighter food future for everyone. We build skills and reinforce the day to day school learning through hands on kitchen knowledge and confidence. Our secondary goal is to brining sustainability to families with time together, and greater health and sense of being in their communities. To become part of our community, and to teach with our curriculum, reach out to us, and we will help you use your skills to reach out to others

A Note from the Chef:

I have a hard time imagining how people were able to share recipes and make their grandmothers' best pies when the instructions were so subjective. I think Fannie would be pleased with the way home cooks everywhere use and understand the need for true measurements, and how well the world has taken on the concept of "food for health" that she began. I'm impressed that she pushed through physical troubles in her life to make a difference in kitchens everywhere. I wonder what she would think about kids cooking now, and how they understand the importance of good food and good measurements. What a game changer she was!

- Chef Arlena

Made in the USA
Columbia, SC
24 January 2022